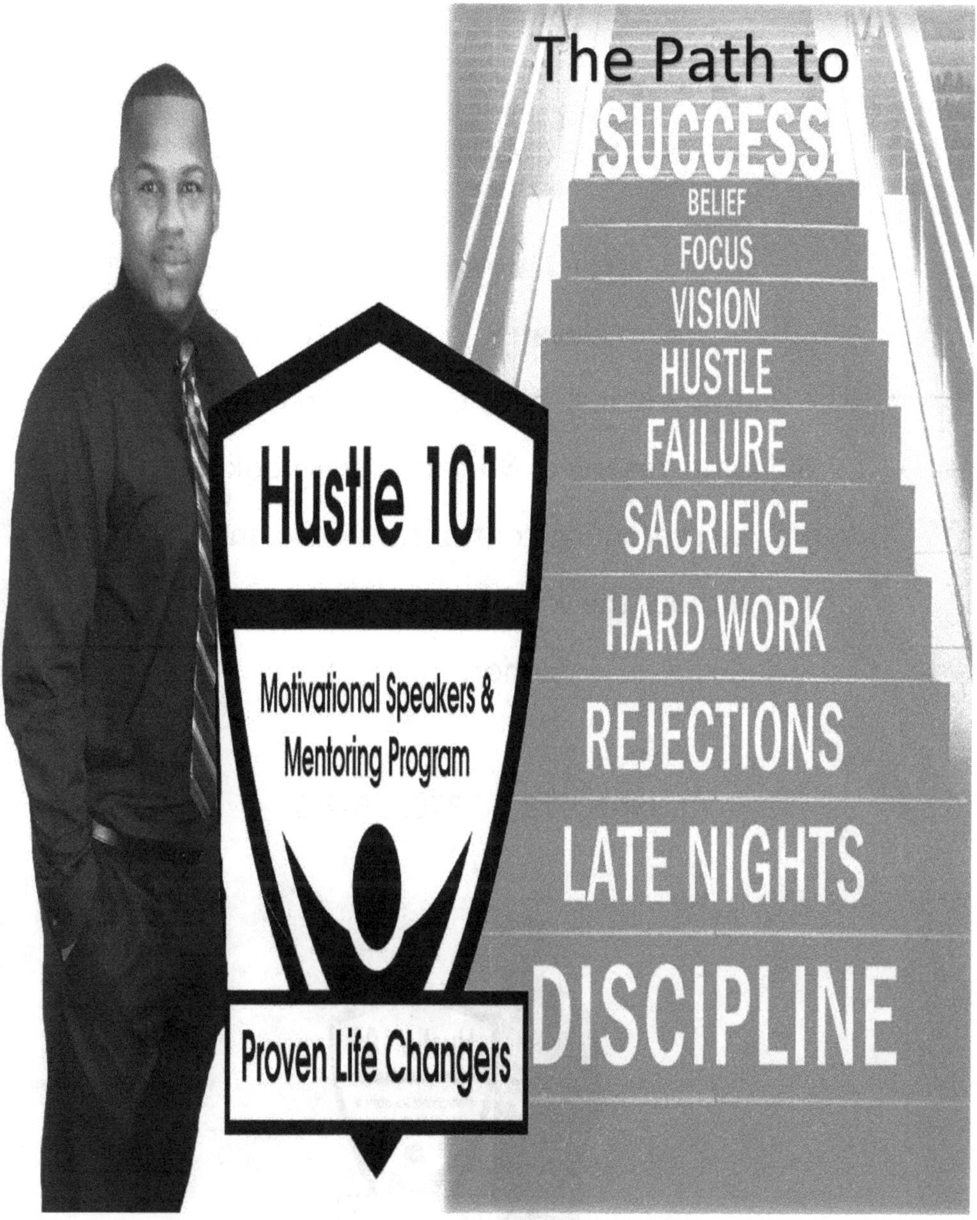
The Path to
SUCCESS
BELIEF
FOCUS
VISION
HUSTLE
FAILURE
SACRIFICE
HARD WORK
REJECTIONS
LATE NIGHTS
DISCIPLINE
Hustle 101
Motivational Speakers &
Mentoring Program
Proven Life Changers

The Path to Success

(There are no elevators on the path to success)

Copyright © 2021 by Santiego Rivers

All rights reserved. No part of this book may be reproduced or transmitted in any form without the written permission of the author.

ISBN 978-1-7370516-2-6

There are no elevators on the path to success! It does not take the money of a rich dad or the knowledge of a poor dad to tell their children about how hard it is to achieve success.

Although it may be challenging to achieve success, it is not impossible for those who are willing to put in the needed work.

Nothing in life that you view as success is easy. With this understanding, you will need to apply the following wisdom:

"If you do what is easy, your life will be hard. But, if you are willing to work hard now, your life will be easy."

Yes, you can win the lottery, inherit money or find some other type of way to come into money, but what you will discover over time is the following:

"A fool and his money will be separated."

This book will explain the steps along the way to the path of success. I will give you examples and personal stories that I had to overcome with each step along my path to success.

I will share the tests that have become my testimony to others about traveling the path to success. I had to learn that if I failed or succeeded in life depended on my mindset and my ability to turn my dreams into reality.

I had to make sure that the obstacles and mistakes I made in my past did not become a life sentence to the "Victory" that I would claim in my future.

My mistakes in the past were only chapters in my book to my path to success. Those mistakes could never tell my whole story. This book will inspire and encourage those to keep traveling on their path to success, one step at a time.

Table of Content

- The power of thinking (pgs. 6-8)
- Discipline (pgs. 9-10)
- Late Nights (pgs. 11-12)
- Rejections (pgs. 13-15)
- Hard work (pgs.16-18)
- Sacrifice (pgs. 19-20)
- Failure (pgs. 21-23)
- Hustle (pgs. 24-26)
- Vision (pgs. 27-28)
- Focus (pg. 29)
- Belief (pgs. 30-31)
- Success (pgs. 32-35)

The power of thinking

As a man thinks, so shall he become. That saying was something that I did not learn as a youth, but I am willing to teach all that is prepared to listen.

It took me years of struggle to learn that everything begins with your thoughts. Rather you think you can, or you think that you can't, you're right.

I struggled with this as a youth and even as an adult. I found myself constantly doing the enemy's work for them by not believing in myself.

I found reasons to doubt myself even when it was no reason present. Self-doubt is the most significant anchor to overcome on your path to success.

I have learned that kids and even adults stop trying to be successful because they feel that it is hard for them to be successful.

If you do not believe that you can achieve success, how can it ever be possible?

It is not what you are that holds you back in life; it's what you think about yourself that holds you back.

Nothing in your life will change until your mind, and your thoughts change. If you don't believe in yourself, why do you think other people will believe in you?

Your dreams, your success awaits you when you decide that you are ready to claim them. When will you be prepared to take that first step?

The first step you will need to take is finally realizing that you are the only author of your destiny. You control the pen, and only you can write the narrative to your story.

What will you write in each chapter in your book? Will your book be about your triumph over the odds you faced, or will your story be about the could've, would've, should've moments that held you back?

What role will you play in your story?

Either you will be you're the villain, or you will be the hero you needed to help you on your path to success. Only you can decide the role that you will play in your life.

Your first step is understanding the power of "Positive" thinking.

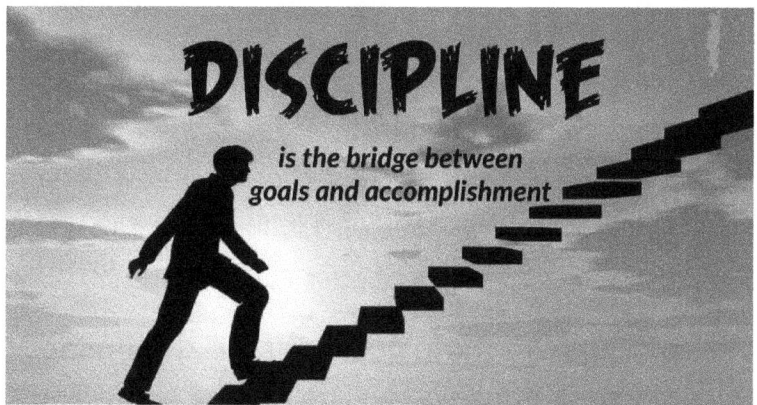

Discipline is what it will take to build that bridge between each step you will take on your path to success.

In your mind, you must develop the mentality that I am built for this. You must believe that you were designed to face and overcome any obstacle you will encounter on your journey to success.

There will be many obstacles along the way to success, so you must become mentally and physically prepared not to give up.

Discipline is being willing to consistently do the small things it will take to overcome significant challenges along your path to success.

Yes, it is the small things that matter the most when you are trying to achieve greatness. I am sorry to inform you that success does not occur overnight.

Success is the by-product of hard work, faith, and discipline. Are you willing to set goals to achieve the things that you want out of life? Are you ready to work hard to achieve those goals even when no one else is watching? Are you willing to keep trying when it seems pointless to continue?

How you answer these questions will determine which type of book you will be writing about your life.

You will either suffer the pain of discipline or suffer the pain of regret. One is only the absents of failing to do the other.

Your motivation to succeed is what will get you going on your path to success. It is going to be your discipline that keeps you going all the way to the end.

Many people will start on the path to success, but not everyone will finish where they hoped. Plato is given credit for saying the following quote:

"The first and best victory is to conquer self."

Will you have the courage to focus on yourself and no one else?

Success may come in the morning, but it starts at night. Successful people are working when everyone else is still sleeping. So, when you wake up in the morning, you are playing catch-up to those people who were working while you were asleep.

In the pursuit of success, the desire to be successful wakes you up out of your sleep and fuels you to keep working even when you're tired.

Successful people understand the following quote:

> *"I will sleep when the job is finish and not when I get tired."*

While you are trying to get your eight hours of rest, someone chasing the same dream you claim you want for yourself is working hard. Those dream chasers are working hard to achieve their goal while you are trying to decide if you wish to work for what you say you want with your words because your actions tell a different story.

"Get your rest, sleeping beauty."

Success is for those willing to go above and beyond or do the *"extra"* it will take to become extraordinary.

These words may sound like a foreign language to some people, but for those who will be successful in their lives, everything that I am saying is making perfect sense.

It will take the power of thinking and discipline to make late nights and early mornings pay off in the end.

For three nights straight, I was awakened out of my sleep. I knew what it meant, but it took that third day for me to get started with my purpose.

My purpose was to write this book. Writing this book is how I spent my late nights and early mornings.

Winners understand the following when it comes to rejection:

"Rejection does not mean that you are not good enough; rejection only means that the other person failed to notice what you have to offer."

Rejection in your life can be the redirection that your life needs. From Thomas Edison to Bill Gates, many successful people had to overcome numerous rejections to get that one "yes" they needed to change their lives.

When one door closes in your life, another door will open for you if you stay ready for the opportunity. Successful people learn to reject rejection and keep pushing forward.

It would be best if you never let a "No" stop you from getting the "Yes" you desire.

To become a Certified Teacher, I had to take the teaching exam several times before I finally passed the test. It would take me a whole year to finally get an opportunity to get a job as a teacher.

I admit that it became frustrating, but I was too focused and determined not to give up on my dreams. I had to put myself in a situation where retreating or quitting was not an option.

I finally landed my dream job. I was teaching in high school and coaching wrestling. Career-wise, I felt that I had made it.

I went from sleeping inside my car as a teacher-aide to finally becoming a certified teacher. I remember when I had to shower at work because I was homeless in a type of way.

I was not making enough to have power or water on at my house

I worked in a different county, and as a teacher aide, I could not afford to commute to work and pay my mortgage at the same time.

I slept inside my car in different locations.

There were times that I wanted to give up and go back to my old ways of making money, but with prayer and discipline, I managed to stick it out and continue to fight for what I wanted to achieve.

I remember my colleagues getting teaching jobs before me and how it made me feel inside. I knew that I was a better teacher than them, but I guess that the Most High was waiting to put me at the location that deserved my talent.

All the tests that I faced along the way to become a certified teacher became the testimony that allowed me to write my first book and share my story with the world.

My first book, "Why I Teach," is my pursuit of success. My book will explain to the reader my path to success and what kept me moving forward even when I felt like giving up.

The readers of my book, "Why I teach," will understand what it takes to achieve your goals and how self-discipline helped me achieve my goals.

The readers of this book will learn to develop a step-by-step plan to achieve their goals in life.

The recipe for success is the following:

Dreams, discipline, hard work & dedication will equal success.

If you are willing to put these ingredients in a pot and give it time, your success is guaranteed. Your dreams will not come true unless you are eager to put in the needed work to make it possible.

You cannot dream your way into having the life that you desire. Once your eyes open, you must develop a plan of action to achieve all the goals you had in your dreams.

You will need to create a vision board to start the process of turning your dreams into reality. After you make your vision board, you must begin to put in the work it will take to accomplish every goal you put on your vision board.

The purpose of the vision board is to get you to start dreaming with your eyes open and put in that work to achieve your goals.

As a child, my grandfather told me two important things when it comes to hard work.

1st, You get what you work for and not what you wish for in life.

2nd, Hard work beats talent when talent doesn't work hard.

I carried these two principles into my adult years, and it has served me well over the years. Hard work is the accountability it will take to be successful in life.

I will never claim to be the most talented or most gifted person, but I will proclaim and prove that you will not outwork me any day.

I am a different type of animal!!!

So, my question to you is, how hard are you willing to work to achieve success in your life? I know that I will do whatever it takes using everything I have inside me.

Are you willing to throw everything you have at all the things you say you want? It will take everything you have to get all the things you say you want.

> "**Hard work** only requires you to do the needed **work** to achieve your goals."

You must be willing to work harder than you did yesterday. And the next day, you must repeat the same process.

You should never be satisfied with your accomplishments because you should be setting new goals every time you conquer one goal.

Please show me a person who is satisfied or content where they currently are at in their life, and I will break down all the reasons why they are not truly living their best life.

Your mindset should be that you are constantly learning and growing from the cradle to the grave.

Sacrifice

Success takes sacrifice, so the question becomes, what are you willing to sacrifice to achieve success?

Sacrifice does not always mean that the circumstances are a life or death situation. It could simply mean that you must be willing to give up something you have to get what you want.

Your sacrifice could be that you give up your time hanging with friends and family to spend extra time working on achieving your goals.

You name a successful person, and I can point out all the things that the person had to give up to achieve their level of success.

If you plan to prosper, you must be willing to walk away from certain situations and people in life.

Chasing my dreams and trying to provide for my family, I sacrificed a lot of things. I forfeited sleeping, sometimes eating, spending quality time with my wife and kids, and doing all the things I wanted to do because I was too busy doing all the things I needed to do to be successful.

I missed many family trips because I was too busy making sure that they had a house to come home to when they returned from their vacation.

When you grow up not having things, you try to make sure that your kids have everything they need. Providing for your family will require sacrifice!

"Success will separate the boys from the men and the women from the girls."

Those people who have achieved success can give you a list of the things they had to give up, including some of the things they wished they could get back.

Time is the most significant sacrifice that you must be willing to make. Your mindset must be that you are ready to sacrifice today to put yourself in a position to reap tomorrow's benefits.

The mindset of a winner is that failure is not an option. If success only requires you to give everything you got, why not give everything you must to achieve everything you want?

"Stop talking about success and start working at being successful."

Your words can lose power when your actions don't match. Learn to replace the wishing game with the doing game and go after your dreams.

Time waits for no one. You must be willing to pick up the pace and be present in the moment. Learn to be present now before the moment passes you by.

What is your reason for you not being successful or at least present in the moment?

If you woke up this morning and you showed up to work or school, then you have work to do!

When it comes to failure, you need to understand that you should never confuse a single defeat with the outcome.

Your **First/Attempt/In/ Learning** is only a lesson to prepare you for each step along the way in achieving success.

Don't be afraid to fail; you should only be terrified not to try. The *effort* is the second step in achieving success. The first step is finding your reason to apply your effort.

You will learn more from your failure than from success. Failure or hitting rock bottom will teach you valuable lessons about yourself that will make you feel like superman when you reach the top.

Who will you discover in your pursuit of success?

To have the life that you desire will require you to become a hustler. Hustling requires conviction. Conviction brings upon transformation.

Hustlers know that if they are not willing to work to be successful, they will fail. The only way to become an overnight success is to hustle every day!

Hustlers know that no nine-to-five job will ever satisfy their wants or needs to have more. Most of nine-to-five jobs only pay you a check or salary that they feel it would take for you not to pursue your dreams.

There are twenty-four hours in a day. You spend eight hours sleeping, eight hours working on somebody else job to help make them rich, so why not use half of those other eight hours to chase your dreams?

I don't think that no one ever dreamed of working a dead-end nine-to-five job as a child. What child do you know says that they envision themselves flipping burgers or bagging groceries as adults?

I know that sometimes circumstances in your life make you do the things you do not want to do until you can do the things you want to do with your life.

Somewhere down the line, most people had to settle for less because they stopped chasing what was best for them.

A hustler thinks the hardest thing to do is not chase their dreams, while a nine-to-five worker feels that chasing their dreams is the most challenging thing to do.

The mindset of a nine-to-five worker:

- What if I fail?
- What if it does not work out?
- What about my job security?
- What about my health care and retirement?

The mindset of a nine-to-five worker:

- I believe in myself, and I refuse not to follow my dreams.
- I am willing to put in the work required to make my dreams come true.
- I don't want to give someone else the best years of my life when they can fire me whenever they feel that my value to the company is no more.
- No one can fire me from my own business or trade because I am a boss and not a worker.
- There are many ways to have health and life insurance without being a nine-to-five worker.
- You can learn ways to save and invest your money for your retirement that do not require you to work as a nine-to-five worker.

The only way to be successful is to make sure of the following:

Your dreams should be more significant than all your fears of failing or not even trying to succeed.

Vision

The scariest thing about chasing your dreams is not when other people do not realize or see your vision. The most frightening thing is when you stop seeing or understanding why you are chasing your dreams.

Your dreams and goals are yours. Other people are not supposed to understand why your dreams and goals are so important to you.

Your hard work and the outcome will make them understand and see why you never gave up on achieving your goals in life.

Your life should be lived by you and not dictated by the thoughts of other people.

Don't let people who knew you back then hold you to be the person you were back when they knew the old version of you that wasn't focused or dedicated to their dreams.

The new version of you decided to apply hard work to the visions you want to manifest into your reality.

The new version refuses to stop trying to be successful even if it offends the people around you.

Your vision will pull you in a direction that refuses to allow you to settle for accepting low expectations in your life and force you to make a dedication to your life dreams.

How badly do you want to achieve your dreams?

There's a big difference between what people say with words and what they mean with actions. Your words will never bring your visions into reality. Your action will make a way even when other people may think differently about your chances.

Your vision fuels your desire never to give up!

Iron sharpens iron. If the people around you are weaker or don't possess the same qualities as you, you will not develop or become the best version of yourself.

Achieving greatness requires you to make many sacrifices, apply dedication, and focus on the vision that drives you.

Your focus is what will determine your reality. So, what are you focusing on? Are you trying to live a life that would please other people or live a life that pleases you?

Once you determine your path to success and apply the discipline and energy to your vision, there will be a time on your journey that your belief in your success will have to be greater than your fear of failing.

The possibility of failing is always a possibility when you are chasing your dreams, but the odds of failure are more significant when you do not try at all. You must dare to be great!

"Who am I to be great?"

Greatness takes conviction, hard work, and focus, including believing in yourself along your path to success.

There were many times on my path to success where I had moments that I wanted to give up because I was afraid that I couldn't achieve my goal.

Looking in the mirror put me in a place where the reflection that I saw was the replication of doubt that I let other people's opinions become the image that I saw in the mirror.

Turning those *"the world vs. me"* moments into a *"me vs. me"* situation gave me the confidence to believe in myself above the doubts of other people who didn't matter when it came to my life.

Looking in the mirror showed me the only person that mattered when it came to my life and achieving the success that I wanted for myself.

It took a lot of tears, overcoming self-doubt, to get to a point where I decided to bite down on my teeth and face all my demons. I had to believe in me if I expected anyone else to see the real me.

I admit it was not always easy, but the outcome was worth it in the end.

My life became a testimony that my belief in myself allowed it to manifest into something beautiful.

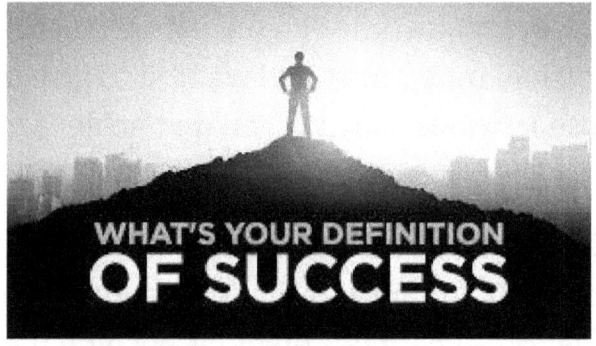

Now is the time that you get the opportunity to write down your definition of success and how you will achieve it every step of the way.

www.ingramcontent.com/pod-product-compliance
Lightning Source LLC
Chambersburg PA
CBHW071339190426
43193CB00042B/2044